IN THE MIDDLE OF THE LINE

Story and Insights By Baruch Talbott

Written By Debby Coughlan

Copyright © 2012 by Baruch Talbott and Debby Coughlan

All rights reserved.

ISBN: 978-1-300-17899-6

DEDICATION

*For my brother, Jerry
and for Samuel, Playboy, and Momobah
who were like brothers to me.*

– Baruch Talbott

*For Mom, who inspired me to write,
and for Dad, who taught me to appreciate
each day's journey.*

– Debby Coughlan

ACKNOWLEDGEMENTS

Many people supported us in this endeavor and for that we are truly grateful. We would like to thank the following people who played a special role in making this book a reality:

Thank you to Rebecca Quinn and her classes at Randolph Macon Academy for reading the first few chapters of our book and providing valuable feedback.

Thank you to Tony Forrest, who read and edited several drafts of the book and was a constant cheerleader.

Thank you to Erin Ford, who reviewed Baruch's written insights and offered helpful comments.

Thank you to our families, especially to David and Naomi Talbott for their support, and to Dean, Matt, Lisa, and Kristin Coughlan for always believing.

We are especially grateful to Kristin Coughlan for creating the original cover design.

CONTENTS

PROLOGUE   13

PART ONE: THEN

1. Hide and Seek   15
2. Social Networking   17
3. Seeing the Light   19
4. Building Bridges   21
5. Love Hurts   23
6. Finding Family   25
7. Time Out   27
8. Fearing Fear Itself   29
9. Rite of Passage   31

INTERLUDE: *To Death, the Liberator*   35

PART TWO: LATER

10	New Digs	37
11	Making the Most of It	40
12	Staying Put	42
13	Reading Between the Lines	44
14	Making Connections	46
15	Hell Breaks Loose	48
16	Day By Day	51
17	Wandering	53
18	The High Price of Gas	56
19	Leaving on a Jet Plane	58
INTERLUDE: *To My Birth Parents*		61

PART THREE: NOW

20	Coming to America	63
21	Welcome Home	66
22	Learning the Ropes	68
23	School Days	71
24	A Growing Family	73

25	Not So Close Knit	76
26	Walls, Doors, and Empty Spaces	78
27	Forming a Bond	80
28	Goodbye Again	82
29	Finding Hope	84
30	You've Got a Friend	87
31	To Be or Not To Be a Geek	90
32	Anchors Aweigh	92
33	Finding Grace in Disgrace	94
34	Making My Way	96
35	Wrestling With Life	99
36	Running the Race	101
37	Deciding Factors	103
38	Making the Most of It, Again	105
39	Continuing the Climb	107
40	Back in the Middle	110

EPILOGUE	113
REFERENCES	115

MESSAGE FOR READERS

Our book was written to capture experience and inspire thought. Although every attempt was made to relate specific details as they occurred, memory becomes clouded through the years, so that non-fiction may become fiction in the blink of an eye. Therefore, some characters and events appearing in this work are fictitious. In those cases, we appreciate your understanding.

PROLOGUE

In life we cannot choose our beginnings; we cannot choose the household and family we are born into. It is God, our parents and guardians that depict where we begin. They strive to set us on a path of success and righteousness.

As we grow up and become adults, we have the freedom and ability to choose to stay on the path of success and righteousness or stray off onto a path of failure and shame. Some of us may not be able to choose what path we take in life because we are not as blessed and free as others, maybe because of the country we live in. But no matter the situation of our lives, we still have the ability and freedom to choose to make the best of what we have.

At some point in our lives we will all face adversities such as the loss of a close friend or family member, unemployment, and racism. We can choose to allow these adversities to hold us down and keep us feeling self pity for what has happened or we can conquer them and see the positive things that come out of them.

Through the death of loved ones we are united to honor them and celebrate their lives. This creates an opportunity for us to reach out to each other in time of need, and create new relationships or strengthen weak ones. Through unemployment we have an opportunity to explore new areas of work and find ourselves. And through racism we are brought together to stand up against those who hate us.

As a child, I watched my life and the people I loved fall around me. But I strove to see all the positive things that came out of the negative things that happened. As you read my story, I hope and pray that it will inspire you to do the same. -- Baruch

Baruch Talbott and Debby Coughlan

THEN - 1

HIDE AND SEEK

I was walking on a dusty road with my uncle when his hand slipped away. In the moment before, I saw movement in the tall grass, remembered stories of wild animals, and stopped to investigate. At the age of three, each image was new to me and I wanted to take in every one. Yet, now I found myself alone in the middle of a dirt road, not knowing which way to turn.

I gazed up and saw nothing but the bright, hot sun. When I looked down, dark gray sand stared back at me. Ahead, the little road meandered through serene farmland and then on to the end of the earth. My uncle was gone, and I was a tiny dot in the midst of an expansive landscape.

The first time it happened, I thought I would be dragged into the towering grasses where the darkness would swallow me alive. Strangely, I felt more alone every time, even though I soon learned exactly what to expect. My uncle took me for walks and then hid in the bushes hoping to lose me, with the same level of concern one gives to misplacing the morning newspaper.

I don't remember how I got there, but when I eventually found my way back to my uncle's house, fear took on other shapes. I was obviously a burden his family didn't need, and they had their own ways of letting me know.

His fourteen-year-old son played a game with me, laughing while he held a gun to my head to see my reaction. I'll never know if that gun was loaded or not, but it had the same effect on me either way.

My earliest childhood memory was also my first encounter with fear. At age three, fear is supposed to be about fretting over a toy that might be grabbed by an older brother.

As an impressionable child in Liberia at the onset of the country's Second Civil War in the late 1990s, fear stared me in the face and left me empty, wanting to be filled with something good.

THEN – 2

SOCIAL NETWORKING

Something good came in the form of Auntie Snoh. She had a kind heart, taking in those who needed her help, and I was fortunate to be one of them. I don't remember how I ended up there, but if my uncle dropped me off, it was the best thing he ever did for me. I'd imagine it's more likely that one of the local townspeople took me there after finding me alone in the middle of a dusty road one day.

I have very few memories about my early days in Liberia but the best and most vivid ones are associated with Auntie Snoh. She was short and plump with very dark skin, and known for her cooking skills. In Liberia, weight was a symbol of wealth, and from the looks of Auntie Snoh, she was rich indeed.

Auntie Snoh's one-story house was blue and red – and large, compared with those around it. Shaded by fruit trees, the front porch had a little wooden bench that was well worn from many folks who had lingered there, waiting to buy fish or smoked deer meat from Auntie Snoh's little store. Sometimes that bench was used as a makeshift barber chair for giving haircuts, or as a place to pause before asking Auntie Snoh for a favor.

I loved the stillness and peace of the little pond behind the house even though the smell of the stagnant water was intense. The well in the yard was our lifeline. Along with our neighbors, it was where we quenched our thirst, cleaned our clothes, and filled our souls. Fear didn't visit the little well – we pumped the smooth, metal handle and it flowed with joy and laughter.

There, in the care of Auntie Snoh, I felt safe and secure. Even her name was ideal; it sounded like *snow*. Although Africans are known for their polite manners, her extraordinary level of kindness was as rare as snowflakes in our land. It would be many years before I would see snow for the first time, but it still fills me with a sense of peace.

At the age of five, nestled in my own room in this familiar little cottage, I began to feel like I belonged. I was at home.

And that's when Auntie Snoh explained that it would be best for me to go to an orphanage. Since I trusted Auntie Snoh – and because, honestly, I didn't have a choice – I went without saying a word.

How I would love to sit on the little bench with Auntie Snoh again today to share what I have learned over the last thirteen years.

THEN – 3

SEEING THE LIGHT

Auntie Snoh was mostly right about my new environment. Days in the African Christian Fellowship International (ACFI) orphanage in Monrovia, Liberia were fun. There were many young kids to play with – about 200 in all – and the adults were usually nice.

We attended church three times a day, and the only difficult part about that was sitting through long sermons. On Sundays, a single service lasted three hours, and if we fell asleep, sometimes they would whip us with a long stick. The pastors were good preachers, but you couldn't expect a bunch of five-, six-, and seven-year-olds to stay awake while old guys were giving long speeches. We looked forward to Sunday School, where the pastor's wife brought Bible stories to life.

We learned to respect older people and never to question authority. Most things were decided for us, including our hairstyles. For boys, that meant shaved heads. The girls suffered a more painful fate, with braids so tight it must have hurt to blink.

The best thing of all was stuffing paper into an old sock and playing soccer with my friends. We would make our own goals by walking off the proper distance and laying shoes or sticks on the ground as markers.

Occasionally, we were lucky enough to have a real soccer ball that someone had shipped over from America. When it arrived, we'd all crowd around the box, and the adults couldn't open it fast enough. We would have kicked the box around until the ball fell out of the wrappings if they would have let us. The only time the ball was not in use was when we were eating, sleeping, or sitting in church, so it would soon pop and we'd be back to stuffing paper in our socks.

There was more to our day than just playing games, and Samuel, John, Playboy, and I developed a gang-group among the little kids. Samuel was dark, shy, and skinny with a big head, and Playboy was the exact opposite – light-skinned, tall and strong. John was somewhere in between. They called me Barry Chea and I became the accepted leader.

The only time I ever remember the gang turning on me was when I accidentally messed up a little flashlight we had worked so hard to make. When it broke in my hands, they shoved my face into the ground and stuck sand in my nose and mouth until I could barely breathe. Although I spent about a week trying to get the sand out, I wasn't angry. I was beginning to understand that respect is a two-way street.

Breaking that flashlight provided me with the glimmer of insight I needed to begin making my way in an uncertain world. When you're a leader, blind followers do you no good. But those who hold you accountable – while still caring about you – help you to become a better person.

THEN – 4

BUILDING BRIDGES

If any of the older boys would pick on us or try to steal our food, I took charge. That meant finding a way to go around a bigger kid and get on his back to bring him down. With that done, we'd climb on him to make sure he wouldn't get loose and come after us. We would take sand and put it in his mouth and beat him good so he'd never mess with us again. Fighting was not for pleasure; it was for self-preservation, and somehow we usually managed to have these skirmishes out of the sight of any adults.

It wasn't always easy, but we stuck together. I couldn't help but bond with people I spent every minute with, and we developed our own solutions for everyday challenges. The best way to cool off on a hot day was to stretch out on the smooth concrete floor. At night, we slept sideways in bed so three or four of us would fit. When we were hungry, occasionally we were lucky enough to knock a bird out of the air with a slingshot. Matches were easy to come by, so we cooked the creature ourselves over an open fire.

Playboy became my bodyguard, helping out when anyone came after me. Although he was one of my best friends, I don't know how Playboy got his nickname. No one ever questioned that because we accepted each other at face value.

One time at night, a big kid beat me up and Playboy wasn't awake to help, so I did my best to defend myself. When Playboy woke up, he made the guy pay for it. That's what friendship was all about. When I cut my finger several days later, the same kid saw my weakness and came after me. This time, I beat him up myself and he never messed with me again.

John and I were good friends, too, and I remember one boring afternoon when the two of us longed to go exploring. We daydreamed about having more freedom and the thought of going anywhere seemed like an adventure.

Without telling the adults, we snuck away to a market next to a lake where we spent the day catching clams. I was astounded at John's willingness to go into the water after all the stories we had heard about sharks and menacing waves that would surely consume us. So, John caught the clams while I watched from the shore but I enjoyed the journey just the same.

As close as I was to my young friends, I managed to bond with the big guys, like Momobah, Austin, and Peter, because I applied the concept of respecting older people to kids as well as adults. The older guys equated my respect with confidence, and over time, they accepted me as a friend. I especially remember Momobah who treated me like his little brother.

Looking back, I realize that I was the bridge between the two groups of kids. Earning the trust of the older guys enabled me to nurture and protect my closest buddies.

THEN – 5

LOVE HURTS

I guess I was one of the lucky kids at the orphanage because aunts and uncles occasionally came to visit me, and that didn't happen for most people. Auntie Snoh often took me back to help in her market and I enjoyed the time at her home, one of the rare dwellings in the village that had electricity.

Once, I got to spend the Christmas holiday at Auntie Snoh's house. During that time, I became friends with the daughter of a half-blind man who rented from her. At the ripe old age of six, I had met the first girl who interested me. I liked her; we hung out a lot, walked to church together, and we went to the well to get water when she helped my aunt cook.

One day, we were sitting by a tree and got into an argument. I don't like to fight, but if I have to, I will. She slapped me and it made me crazy; I punched her back and quickly discovered she was pretty good at fighting. I'm not sure who came out ahead but she scratched my face so I had to explain things to my aunt.

Next thing I knew, Auntie Snoh had kicked the girl's family out of the house and I never saw her again. I can't say which was worse: the embarrassment of being beaten up by a girl, or the loneliness I felt when she was gone.

With the holidays long over, my aunt took me back to the orphanage but I had stayed away too long and they were reluctant to let me back in. Orphanages were reserved for those who were truly desperate. If some of us could live with relatives, there was no shortage of kids to fill the beds we left behind.

Auntie Snoh graciously offered to keep me with her, but I think there was uncertainty about how long that could last. In the end, the orphanage opened its doors and I was actually relieved to be back in the comfort of my little group of friends. It might be hard for others to understand, but the orphanage had become home for me.

Home was where my friends were.

I didn't know it until much later, but that narrow escape back *into* the orphanage was a life-changer for me.

THEN – 7

TIME OUT

Despite his peculiar ways, I connected with Jerry as often as possible, starving for a sense of family to call my own. I valued the blood bond we shared and protected it like a cherished gem.

Later that year, when I was playing soccer with my friends, I saw a group of adults coming our way. The adults motioned to me, so I stopped playing and tossed the ball back to my friends. As they moved closer, I suddenly felt compelled to run away.

My feet wouldn't move.

At that moment, it seemed as if a penalty had been committed and someone called time out. Everything around me stopped, except for the solemn people-parade that kept moving toward me. They came so close that I couldn't miss the tears in their professional adult eyes. Sound broke through the silence and I heard only words, but not complete sentences. "Malaria . . . rushed to the hospital . . . the doctors tried, but . . ."

That day, I lost the only immediate family member I truly knew, along with a big chunk of my own heart. As soon as I grew close to Jerry, malaria stepped in and ripped him away from me. I realized he had always been sick, but eight years old and he was gone in an instant! No funeral, no information about his burial, nothing.

Time stopped and my world changed.

I know it's devastating for anyone to lose a relative, but Jerry and I were a fragile family of two small souls, reduced to one trembling silhouette in the blink of an eye. There I was again, a tiny dot on a landscape that seemed larger than life.

That night, with tears streaming down my face, I felt more alone than I had ever been.

I was an island once more.

THEN – 8

FEARING FEAR ITSELF

After that, the concept of death consumed me and I convinced myself that I would be the next to go. It made sense, right? My older brother had died, so I was next in line and that terrified me. My uncle came to the orphanage and tried to make me understand about Jerry, but I wasn't hearing it. I spent the next several days walking alone amid a crowd of silent thoughts.

The quiet pounded in my head as time passed.

On one particular day, I was in a classroom at the school, gazing over at our little church. That simple structure had become the center of our life in the orphanage and perhaps it gave me some comfort.

Suddenly, I heard a deep voice coming from above. When I looked up, I saw nothing, just as I did when I was walking with my uncle at the age of three. But something was different now. The voice became clearer and clearer, as if someone were right next to me, but no one was there. Shaking in fear, I remembered the Bible stories from the pastor's wife and wondered if God was trying to talk to me. Was that really possible?

I wasn't sure, so I turned away, scared out of my mind, but I couldn't escape the deep voice. It called my name, saying, "Barry Chea, you'll be fine." I desperately wanted to find relief in the message but the sound still frightened me because it was obvious that I was completely alone. Was someone messing with me?

I ran away from the school as fast as I could but the voice followed me. I later found some adults and begged them to take me back to my room.

At the time, I was too frightened to think. Looking back, there are so many questions I'd like to ask that voice. "How do you know I'll be fine?" "Where are my parents?" and "Why am I here?" Most of all, "Why did Jerry have to die?"

Trembling in my bed later that evening, my mind raced and imminent death was the only thing I could conclude. With no other choice, I responded by bowing my head in prayer, something I still do every day.

Looking back, I realize that was the day God and I truly met.

THEN - 9

RITE OF PASSAGE

The only thing that got me through those next few days was my group of friends who were always there for me. With them, I could forget my fears and feel at home again. We played soccer, hide-and-seek, and tag, or hung out and got into occasional fights. Life slowly started to feel normal again.

About a month later, without notice, my birth mother appeared at the orphanage, along with a man and a boy named Aaron. Apparently, the man was my father's brother and the boy was his son, but in my heart, I believed they were my own father and brother.

Aaron was very dark-skinned, and with similar features, he could pass as my twin. His sudden appearance with these people spooked the adults at the orphanage because at the time they knew I was away at the beach chasing sand crabs with friends. After they finally realized that Aaron and I were not one and the same, the adults came to the beach to get me. When we returned, they let me have a meal with my family – *my family* – just as life was supposed to be. I smiled inside and felt a small sense of comfort.

Perhaps I was not an island after all.

Still haunted by Jerry's recent death, I was intrigued to meet other blood relatives, and proudly introduced Aaron to my friends. He followed me around the school that afternoon and looked up to me just like a kid brother would.

That evening, without warning, the visitors pressed some money into my hand, told me to spend it on whatever I wanted, and left with Aaron as quickly as they had arrived. Just like that, more acquaintances had walked into my life and tried to pass as family.

That single day is the only memory I have of the people who were my closest relatives. I haven't seen them since.

Several weeks later, most of the boys in the orphanage were instructed to decide if we wanted to be circumcised. At age seven, this concept was completely foreign to me so I made my decision by talking to other guys who said it wasn't bad at all. I bravely got in line, having no idea what to expect. The kids must have taken great joy in playing a dirty trick on me because it was the most horrific pain I have ever endured and it is surely one that I will never forget.

Soon after that, one of the adults in the orphanage took me for a walk and explained that, a while ago, someone in the village had shot and killed my father. If true, it would dash the hope that the mysterious man who appeared with my mother might have been my dad. Perhaps my mother had wanted to tell me this but couldn't bear to break the news.

Void of emotion, I cried a little but it wasn't as bad as it felt with Jerry because I never had the chance to know my father.

With news that another family member had perished, death again consumed my thoughts.

Other than that, it was just another day.

Baruch Talbott and Debby Coughlan

INTERLUDE

TO DEATH, THE LIBERATOR

I've heard stories of all the pain you bring into people's lives. I've heard of how you leave many people with broken hearts, broken promises and destroyed dreams. I've heard of how you leave many innocent children homeless and without a family. I've heard of all the civil strife you've caused.

Now I hear you coming from afar. Little by little, you approach my door. As I watch you approach, my body begins to shake in fear and turns numb. I fear that you have not come for me but for my brother who lies ill and weak in bed. Unable to move, I try to force out words but it seems my fear has sealed my lips and locked away any sound I attempt to make.

As I force my body to turn, I see you kneeling by my brother's body. Shaking in fear, I force myself to move closer to you. I notice my brother's eyes are closed and his body looks lifeless. I fall to my knees and begin to cry but in my heart I know my brother is now at peace. You came to liberate him from all of his pain and suffering.

REST IN HEAVENLY PEACE, JERRY.

-- Baruch

Baruch Talbott and Debby Coughlan

LATER – 10

NEW DIGS

My time back at the orphanage was short-lived because sometime in 2001 or 2002 we were quickly moved to new surroundings in Dixville, where there were twice as many kids. Although we didn't know it, war was raging outside, and apparently staying on the move provided some hope for safety.

More than ten years earlier, Charles Taylor, a former high-ranking official in the Liberian government, had organized armed forces in an effort to overtake the regime of Samuel Doe, resulting in the First Liberian Civil War. Taylor formed the National Patriotic Front of Liberia (NPFL), and a breakaway rebel force known as the Independent National Patriotic Front of Liberia (INPFL) was allegedly responsible for the torture and death of Doe. Amid the fighting, various groups terrorized and killed thousands of innocent Liberian citizens.

In 1997, Charles Taylor became president of Liberia, ushering in a continued reign of terror. It was said that Taylor had participated in guerrilla training under Muammar Gaddafi, and he was sometimes linked to blood diamond activities that involved selling illegal arms to rebel groups in Sierra Leone.

During the late 1990s and early 2000s, the Second Liberian Civil War was well underway. Fighting escalated daily as various rebel groups struggled to overthrow Taylor's corrupt government.

And there we were, caught in the middle, without even knowing it.

Soon after arriving at the new orphanage, I found myself sitting in a little jail cell, its rough cement walls engulfing me in loneliness. While this space would have been intimidating for an adult, it was downright terrifying to an eight-year-old kid. At least there was an opening with bars so I could see some daylight.

At the new facility, fighting was not tolerated, and we had to be careful not to get caught. I only made that mistake once and that's how I ended up in the little cell. For some reason, the adults at the orphanage took pity on me and let me out after only thirty minutes. The other guys were not so lucky, often staying a day or two in that hot dark space with no food at all.

Ironically, even with the threat of the jail cell, there were more fights in the new orphanage than the old one. Perhaps we were growing older and more restless.

Outside the little cell, life in the second orphanage was still depressing. I missed some of the older boys who were forced to stay behind at ACFI because the adults didn't want them interacting with the older girls who came with us. They were afraid that dangerous adolescent combination would produce additional babies, and the last thing we needed was another orphan.

Even though I knew it was a long shot, I spent every night praying that I would be adopted. Mail time was the most popular part of the day, when lucky ones among us received letters, pictures, and money from interested sponsors. Aching inside, I watched, as one by one, others left to live with families in America. I was happy for them, but the pictures they sent back of their new heftier, healthier selves made me even more jealous.

One of the first to leave was a light-skinned girl who was a good friend of mine. She and I used to play soccer together and our nights were spent hanging out, telling African myth stories we had learned from older people. When she left, life was quieter and lonelier, and that made me pray even harder.

With more friends leaving, I was reminded that my brother and father had died recently. I searched for a sense of belonging.

LATER – 11

MAKING THE MOST OF IT

I joined a singing group to pass the time and the members became some of my best friends. The most uplifting part of our day was spent acting in skits and plays, and although we didn't really know it at the time, we were learning a lot along the way.

I found it easy to memorize Bible verses and stories from a guy named Russia King, who originally came to the orphanage to teach us about America. For some reason, he took it upon himself to make sure we were all okay, and in the process, he became like a father to us. He showed us a movie about Jesus being nailed on the cross. Russia King's fire-and-brimstone stories shaped our young perspectives as we hung on his every word.

Although I liked being part of it all, fear confronted me again in the midst of those powerful tales and it was hard sometimes to separate life from acting. We performed compelling stories like *Shadrach, Meshach, and Abednego* and *Daniel and the Lion's Den*, complete with authentic costumes and unique sound effects.

The most frightening account was about Judgment Day and the importance of having your name written in the Book of Life. In the story, people didn't always believe in God, but they were scared to death of Hell. Those who were good would be on the right-hand side of God and their names would appear in the Book of Life. One terrified guy in the story kept pleading for the angel to look harder and harder for his name in the Book until, amazingly, she finally found it. The tale ended with this huge man doing cartwheels because he was so excited that his name was found.

I'm not sure if I'll ever shake that image. Maybe that's why I still choose to express my faith in an internal way, rather than with arms flailing.

The good times didn't last long. Russia King left us as quickly as he had entered our lives. We woke up one day to learn that he had died. We had no idea what happened.

But just like that he was gone.

LATER – 12

STAYING PUT

Death was becoming part of everyday life. It meandered in and out of every place we went, touching family, friends, and acquaintances. Charles Taylor wielded a lot of power, and orphanages must have been ripe recruiting grounds for his militant forces.

One day, a random kid appeared at the orphanage and his presence seemed to alarm the adults, prompting them to call the police. In those days, it was hard to tell the good guys from the bad, and suspicions always ran wild. In the end, the adults decided the kid was a spy, so I think the police killed him. Based on what happened later, I'm pretty sure they were right. Our pastor prayed for that kid's soul, but we heard that he was later eaten by townspeople who were cannibals. I think they told us that to scare us into obedience. It worked.

Fear at times was a tool, and we were easily manipulated.

In the Middle of the Line

When we heard that one of our cooks was killed on her way home from work with her body later found in pieces, we accepted the news without flinching even though it tore us up inside. Bad things were getting close, and judging from the yelling and gunfire we heard constantly beyond our gates, we couldn't help but feel that we would be next to experience the effects.

In the midst of this chaos, we tried to continue with our songs and skits, as I watched many of my new friends from the singing group escape to America. They were some of my closest confidants and it was hard to say good-bye, over and over again. As I stoically recited the familiar farewell song, my heart longed to join them – especially when I witnessed the terror growing around me.

Yet, something big was happening that dominated my attention.

LATER – 13

READING BETWEEN THE LINES

Without Russia King and the singing group in my life, days were long and boring. Other than religion classes, our education was mainly focused on learning a few letters and numbers, including our times tables up to ten.

Some kids communicated in tribal languages, but most of us just spoke pigeon English. A cousin once told me that I was part of the Kru tribe from the southeast part of Liberia, but I never learned about the customs or special language that went along with it. I later heard that the Kru dialect is known for one of the most interesting tone systems in Africa and now I wish I had mastered that.

My spirits were lifted occasionally when the mail came. I had been getting pictures and letters from an American sponsor named Katie who communicated with kids in orphanages and helped to provide money for food, clothes, and mosquito nets. We desperately needed all of those things. Since I couldn't read, Momobah recited the letters aloud and composed responses for me when I wrote back. The words and pictures filled me with happiness.

One day, I received a package from an American family that included a big science book about animals, and I remember it had a cool picture of a snake with two heads. The images made me smile but I didn't really have any use for the book since the words were foreign to me. I passed it along to Momobah and went on with my day.

I didn't know why I was getting those letters and pictures, but I was pretty sure some people in America had seen a picture of me and liked what they saw.

I could only hope – and pray harder.

LATER – 14

MAKING CONNECTIONS

Soon, a kind man named Joseph took me to his house to tell me the news I had spent my life praying for. It appeared that I was being adopted.

In a few days, I found myself talking on the phone with the people in America who had, indeed, liked my picture. I was in church when they called and the pastor came to let me know. Considering the gravity of this long-anticipated phone call, I remember how heavy the black receiver felt in my small hand.

My first conversation was with the dad who seemed especially interested in me. The people on the phone were definitely excited, but I couldn't understand them very well. I just listened with my heart pounding and said "yeah" every now and then, fearful that if I said more, they might change their minds about me.

They described their house and boat and later sent me pictures of their family. I studied every image, and marveled at the fact that the people who could become my mom and dad actually looked very much like each other.

When I hung up, my friends surrounded me in joy and laughter. Surely this remarkable call could only mean I really was being adopted. Although we were young, we all understood the blessing of adoption, despite the bittersweet separation that accompanied it.

That night my pillow felt a little softer and my fears began to fade. Little did I know that life outside our walls was becoming increasingly violent.

Soon, real fear would be knocking – no, pounding – on our door.

LATER – 15

HELL BREAKS LOOSE

I didn't have long to rest in the comfort of my possible adoption. In the days that followed, fear took up residence in our dormitory, and all thoughts of a happier life in America had to be put on hold.

One unforgettable day we found ourselves hiding from guerrilla soldiers who had let themselves in, carrying RPGs, AK47s and machetes. It appeared that they were followers of Charles Taylor, and their huge knives terrified me. I'd heard stories about terrorists who asked people if they wanted a short sleeve or a long sleeve; it was their way of determining where to slice off the arm.

Eight of us shook in fear under a bed as we watched the feet of the guerrillas shuffle past. The night before, half of us had been sleeping in that bed and now we were using it as a security blanket. A friend of mine couldn't hold out any longer and had to get up to go to the bathroom. Next thing we knew, he was lying on the ground in a pool of blood and the impassioned troops were ordering us out from under the beds, shouting that they'd shoot us all.

In the Middle of the Line

In the mayhem that followed, they lined us up against the wall like criminals and took our shoes and clothes – truly the only possessions we had. I was in the middle of the line when a menacing warrior put a gun to my head and ordered me to give him my shoes. He towered over me, and at nine years old, I was petrified. Time stood still as I felt the gun's cold, unforgiving metal against my head.

I didn't move, or blink, or breathe.

Suddenly, the monster turned and fired at kids on the far ends of the line. Before I could react, another militant shot back at me. The gunfire passed by my trembling legs.

The horror seemed to go on forever and the sound of gunshots, screaming, and crying was deafening. When the soldiers took a break, those of us who remained were marched into the chapel along with the pastor.

Shaking in fear, I was glad to be back in that sanctuary. If I had to die, let it be within the walls of our humble little church. Surely God would find me there. We put our throbbing heads on each other's shoulders and prayed. Despite our own fears, we thanked God for the people around us, remembering those who had just died.

And then we came right out and asked God to save us.

I didn't understand why these people wanted to hurt us, but I think it was their way of recruiting new members for their aggressive group that was struggling to maintain power. Orphans are young, impressionable, and easily manipulated.

I remembered the spy who had been to our orphanage a few weeks earlier and was angered that his counterparts had succeeded in attacking our sense of family at the orphanage. They took our possessions, but it was becoming clear that they couldn't steal our resolve.

Later that day, the adults prepared a huge meal that none of us could eat. The bitterness of war simmered in the food. Sick to my stomach, I can't remember the next time I was able to keep anything down.

Faith was my only nourishment and it left me mostly weak.

LATER – 16

DAY BY DAY

The horror wasn't over yet, and eating was the least of my worries. The militants came back the next day and interrupted our afternoon church service. They beat Pastor Sieh until he was unrecognizable. All the while, he bravely stood up for us, pleading for God's grace.

As the insurgents terrorized the other adults, they quizzed each of us kids about our tribes. Our answers to those questions about our heritage were literally a matter of life and death. No amount of studying could have prepared us for such a gruesome test. Samuel was like my little brother, and I held his thin frame as we prayed, avoiding all the questions. I was determined to make sure nothing happened to him.

Then, miraculously, one of the high-ranking soldiers told the others to stop shooting, and silence filled the sanctuary. I wanted to savor the unexpected quiet but could find no solace in it. My watchful eyes were trained on this solitary man who held our fate in his hands.

I braced myself for a frightening trick. Then, for some odd reason, he began telling jokes about the tribes, and his previously impassioned counterparts seemed to appreciate a break from the work at hand. We all took notice, but the eerie quiet and mysterious attempt at humor didn't relieve our fear.

The man's inexplicable action saved many of us that day, including our heroic pastor.

The laughter was short-lived. Soon the troops stormed outside, turned their weapons toward our building, and demolished the entire back portion where we kept our bicycles. I don't know why we were spared, but the guy with the jokes is the only thing that saved the bike riders from being destroyed along with all the bikes that day.

Getting no sleep at all, I continued to panic. The persistent pounding of my heart replaced the day's earlier commotion. I prayed that I wouldn't die, buoyed by the hope of an adoption that now felt so far away.

LATER – 17

WANDERING

Over the next several days, we scrambled from building to building, trying to stay away from the monsters, managing to sleep off and on amid gunshots, screaming, and shouting. They ultimately found us wherever we went, threatening to kill us all if we didn't keep moving. It was their way of controlling us.

We constantly packed up everything we had, prepared to jump at a moment's notice. When the soldiers shouted, "Run!" I hoisted Samuel on my back and sprinted, dodging bullets at my feet. My eyes refused to focus on the lifeless bodies that fell around me. Samuel was so thin that his body was not much different than carrying a backpack, but no weight in the world would have stopped me from lifting him through that nightmare.

Before long, the militants ordered us to walk in a straight line, complimenting some of the bigger kids on their strength and encouraging them to show their manhood by trying out the guns on their friends. From the looks of some of the soldiers' young faces, perhaps many of them had been recruited in a similar way. Horrified, most of my friends ignored the taunts without losing their own lives.

I assumed we were in search of a new building that might provide safety, and the battling forces were intervening every step of the way. We were captive in that line for days as the insurgents swarmed around us like mosquitoes unleashed in a home with no nets. Truckloads of soldiers would pass by throughout the day and several others marched at our side, shouting and shooting at will.

I held out hope, reminded of the Bible story about Jews in search of the Promised Land. I was afraid the sinister men would target Samuel because I was carrying him on my back, so I did my best to blend into the background. Losing Samuel would mess me up for life.

As we trudged along one afternoon, a group of militants stormed out of the bushes and beat our little dog until it was dead. This wasn't just any dog – it was a loyal friend that had been with us since the beginning of time. He was an innocent member of our family, providing happiness while requiring nothing in return. Tears ran down our expressionless faces when we realized that the heartless monsters had likely eaten the poor creature. We never saw our beloved pet again.

I was quickly learning that it wasn't a good idea to get close to anyone or anything, because those you loved could be destroyed in an instant. I was helpless to change that.

One night we hunkered down in a random building infested with rats that nibbled the skin off our feet while we slept. I was amazed that this tickling feeling was almost soothing compared with the nightmare we had endured over the past several weeks.

The next day we were put on a bus en route to a hotel, or perhaps an abandoned government building. Making several trips, the bus had to pass directly between the combatants, with troops on one side and opposing rebels on the other. One brave adult risked his own life by convincing each side to briefly stop shooting as we gingerly zigzagged between. I don't know how we made it through, but thankfully, Samuel was still at my side.

Inside our new fortress, we were shielded from the horror beyond and only had glimpses of the machine-gun-clad militants or opposing rebels when the gates were opened for delivery trucks to enter or leave. Yet, those gates couldn't ward off the sounds of war: shouting, shooting, shrieking, shouting, shooting, shrieking.

With that backdrop, a simple soccer game became impossible.

LATER – 18

THE HIGH PRICE OF GAS

Days at our makeshift home blended together until one memorable moment when a strange man walked up to me and asked for my name. When I responded, he reached for my hand and told me to follow him. The next thing I knew, the man handed a stack of papers to the pastor and we were out the door.

I couldn't help but think that the pile of papers represented my freedom. Remembering my phone conversations with the interested family in America – and shuddering at the horrific events of the last several months – I followed along in blind faith.

I jumped into the back seat of a car with only the clothes on my back and a small woven bag containing a jar of Blue Magic hair grease. The calm man seemed nice enough, so I wasn't afraid – until our car suddenly stopped in the middle of the countryside.

The man and his driver departed, leaving me alone inside. As the silence persisted, I sank down in the seat, wondering what to do.

In the Middle of the Line

Perhaps this was a big mistake. Could I sneak back to the orphanage?

Just then, gunshots filled the air. Terrified, I pressed my body into the bottom of the car, melting into a dirty, boiling floorboard that was soaked with sweat and tears. A flurry of people ran around the car. I was sure the two men were dead and I would be next.

Miraculously, they returned as quickly as they had departed. We were again on our way, as if nothing had happened.

Our travels were soon cut short again by a group of soldiers who pointed their guns at the car and insisted they would shoot us on the spot unless we gave them money for the small bottle of gas they waved at us. I was relieved when the man paid them but the agitators kicked our car, yelled some more, and then tormented us for many miles before they finally disappeared.

I never understood exactly what occurred that day, but I had become accustomed to strange circumstances. Asking questions never seemed to help a situation.

In fact, I knew from experience that it was usually best to keep quiet.

LATER – 19

LEAVING ON A JET PLANE

As it turned out, the man who had taken me from the orphanage was Emmanuel Wureh, an important leader associated with the Liberian Supreme Court. He was especially kind, and his home felt like a mansion. I stayed with him for about two weeks, and he fed me until I could eat no more.

The day finally came when Mr. Wureh took me to the airport, where we met up with other orphans who were headed to Ghana to connect with adoptive parents. Due to the war, Americans were discouraged from traveling to Liberia since there was no way to ensure safety.

The other children at the airport included a baby named Tucker who was missing fingers and limbs as the result of an attempted abortion. When Tucker's caretaker asked me to hold him, I was terrified, and the baby responded by poking me in the eye with his only finger. Looking back, I have to laugh at myself for being afraid of a tiny baby who, at the time, showed more confidence than I did.

In the Middle of the Line

God must have given Tucker a special sense of humor to help him compensate for the challenges he would face in life through no fault of his own.

Tucker wasn't the only one who had been disfigured. Gazing at the people around the airport, I concluded that the stories I'd heard about the machetes were true. I saw a man press a fistful of money into the pocket of a person who was missing an arm and a leg.

As we boarded the plane, I held my little woven bag with one hand and clutched my buttonless pants with the other to keep them from falling down. Shuffling along, I squeezed the toes on my left foot to hold my broken flip flop in place.

The next thing I knew, we had landed in Ghana where a slim, smiling man with salt-and-pepper hair was running up to me with open arms. He looked older than his picture but it didn't matter. It had been a long journey, but finally, there he was, right in front of me.

Letting go of my pants and bag, I fell into his arms.

Dad.

Baruch Talbott and Debby Coughlan

INTERLUDE

TO MY BIRTH PARENTS

Isaiah and Eva,

I thank God every day for you giving me life, even though our time together was cut short. Although you are not with me in a tangible form, I know that you are with me in spirit and that you are guiding me through life.

Right now, I'm in the middle of an incredible journey, but I look forward to the day when we will all be together as a family and never be separated again.

-- Baruch

NOW – 20

COMING TO AMERICA

The flight to America was a whole new experience for me. Due to numerous delays, my dad's round-trip ticket had long expired, and the only way we could leave without waiting several weeks was to fly first-class from Accra to Amsterdam. It took so long to process all the immigration papers that we would have missed this flight, too, if my dad had not handed a few dollars to the guard who took us directly to a high-ranking official.

The official processed my paperwork himself before Dad and I raced through the airport to catch our plane. Someone must had tipped off the flight attendants, because when we arrived at the gate out of breath, they shouted, "You made it!" and hustled us on the plane.

We were the last two people to board the aircraft. I immediately looked around, wide-eyed. I had never seen so many white people in my life and I found myself staring at their fair complexions and light hair.

We were as different as night and day on the outside, and so far I knew nothing about Americans on the inside. They seemed nice enough, giving me peanuts and soda, which I had never tasted before. As it turned out, the kindness of the crew and first-class passengers was wasted on me because I felt pretty sick through most of the flight.

During a layover in Amsterdam, my dad bought me a pair of Timberland boots and I was relieved to walk without squeezing my toes together. When we stopped by the bathroom before boarding our connection to America, I had to be reminded to use toilet paper since it had rarely been available to me when we were on the move in Liberia.

It was a long flight to America with plenty of time to think. I became fearful of the new place I was about to encounter. America had been described to me as heaven, but I had no idea what that meant.

My mind wandered back to the country I was leaving behind. I thought of Samuel, Playboy, and Momobah, and wondered what they were doing at that very moment. I imagined them moving from place to place and marching amid gunfire. Who would be there to carry Samuel through? I squeezed my eyes closed and winced at the thought, feeling guilty that I was being treated like a king on an airplane while they were likely in search of their next hiding place and too scared to eat – if they were still alive.

And then I thought about the few family members I had come to know in Liberia. The adoption papers indicated that my father was dead and my mother had disappeared. I don't know if all that's true but I understood that those details were required for my adoption to go through. Did Aaron disappear too? Was he my brother or my cousin?

I wondered if I would ever see any of them again. Was I running away, or being pulled toward something?

The orphanage had notified Auntie Snoh and my uncle about the adoption, but I didn't get the chance to say goodbye to either of them. For a moment, I imagined myself perched on the little bench on Auntie Snoh's porch, safe in the comfort of her familiar home.

And then I drifted off to sleep.

When I awoke, the plane was landing and my heart was pounding. Here I was, arriving in the United States, and I didn't know what to expect. At Dulles Airport, I followed the other passengers off the plane and soon saw my blonde-haired sister, Kelly, and my mom amid a crowd of people.

On the way home, we drove right through Washington, D.C., the capital of my new country. I gazed out the window and saw towering monuments that dominated a huge city. I would later learn that those striking structures honored leaders of a very different government than the one I had left behind.

Moments later, I was home.

Home. That sounded so good, although I wasn't yet sure what it meant or how it would feel. Despite all the spaces I had occupied in my life, I had never been in a place called my Home.

NOW – 21

WELCOME HOME

When I arrived home, we measured my height and weight in inches and pounds; both came in at 51. In the weeks that followed, I met the rest of my instant family, which seemed to be overrun with girls. While Kelly was just two years older, my other blonde-haired sisters, Katie and Kristin, had already graduated from high school. With my jet-black skin and dark eyes, I felt like the complete opposite of my sisters. Even my name didn't fit into the alliterative bond shared by Katie, Kristin, and Kelly.

Although I felt happy inside, no one knew it because fear was still my companion. Perhaps it wasn't really happiness I was feeling. At this point, it seemed more like relief with a small dose of insecurity. Based on past experience, I certainly wasn't ready to risk the devastating pain of getting close to family members who might die or disappear.

As fate would have it, our home was located on a small peninsula that jutted into a river near Annapolis, Maryland. That scared me to death because I had been told that waterways contained all kinds of terrible creatures. My days at the orphanage flashed through my mind and I remembered the adults sternly warning us to stay away from open water with wild fish that would eat us alive.

To make matters worse, I had arrived in Maryland just days after the remnants of a hurricane hit, and our back yard was flooded. My eyes widened like the water that drew ever closer to our house.

When my dad expected me to help with clearing debris from the waterlogged yard, I was frustrated. From everything I had heard, America was all about freedom. People in Liberia even referred to this place as *the good life*. I thought that meant I wouldn't have to work while I was here, but I soon learned otherwise. On the contrary, my dad made a regular habit of assigning endless chores to me.

One evening, my dad and I watched *Roots* together and I was introduced to the concept of racism. The images in the movie were strikingly real, leading me to believe that I must have been brought to America to be a slave. My theory would certainly explain why so many Americans were lined up to adopt deserted Liberian kids like me. I took that to heart and concluded that my chores seemed much more demanding than those given to my sister Kelly, even though she was two years older and quite capable. When I finally voiced these thoughts, my parents seemed genuine in their denial, but I wasn't ready to accept their words.

I had been so excited about coming to America and now it was the source of new fears that were becoming increasingly complicated.

NOW – 22

LEARNING THE ROPES

One of my first memories upon arriving in America was the people – so many of them everywhere, smiling and talking and laughing and wanting to know me. My parents had good intentions, taking me around to meet all the neighbors and introducing me to friends at church. I didn't say a single word to any of them. Still in shock, I had decided that talking might lead to trouble and I wasn't going to take any unnecessary chances in this strange new place.

Exasperated at my stubborn refusals to utter a word in public, my dad finally came up with the idea of paying me money to talk to people, and the plan actually worked. Even though I had no real use for the cash, I liked the challenge of *getting* something in return for *doing* something. Best of all, it made me feel like I was in control, something I had never known. I justified my actions by convincing myself that I might someday send a portion of that money back to Liberia. And, when Hurricane Isabel devastated our area in 2003, I emptied my wallet for the cause.

I was excited when my parents signed me up for a soccer team, until I realized that winter was just barely over. My fingers tingled from the icy cold, and my thin legs trembled as I stood on the field. Although we had our share of troubles in Liberia, weather was not one of them. We had just two seasons: dry or rainy. Cold was a hindrance we didn't have to endure. Disillusioned, I was quickly learning that America was not as perfect as everyone had said.

A bright spot during that time was meeting James, one of my first friends in America. Hanging out with him felt comfortable, like being in the company of Samuel, John, and Playboy. James and I were on the same soccer team, and I think we lost every game that year. Despite my days of playing soccer in the orphanage, I was unaccustomed to the organized version of the game and wasn't much help on my new team. I'm embarrassed to say that, on one occasion, I think I even scored a goal for our opponent.

Talking to people and learning about organized sports were just a few of the challenges I faced in my new surroundings. I was now part of a boating family, and like it or not, water was something I would have to endure. One day, we were heading out on the family boat for a weekend of exploration on the Chesapeake Bay. Just as the boat reached the mouth of the South River, I stared at the water and started screaming from my perch, "Nemo's teacher, Nemo's teacher!" After spotting that real-life version of the stingray I had seen in the animated movie, I wouldn't go near the water for the rest of the weekend.

Woods terrified me as much as water, for I was sure they were filled with snakes. I cried uncontrollably when my family tried to take me out on hikes until I discovered the safety of an asphalt trail at Quiet Waters Park in Annapolis. After I became comfortable with the trail, my dad carried me into the woods in an attempt to help me overcome my fear. Squirming in his arms, I beat him until he could hold on no longer. When he dropped me, I ran back to the trail and didn't stop until I reached the parking lot.

Despite my parents' efforts to bond with me, I gravitated toward my small group of friends at every opportunity. The more James and I hung out, the more I trusted him and old fears began to slip slowly away.

I was also becoming good friends with Cory, a soccer teammate whose family was close to ours. Cory's house was like a second home for me, and he became my best friend. In fact, to say that we were friends is an understatement; we did everything together. There were times when my friendship with Cory was the only thing that got me through the day. When his family later moved to Pennsylvania, it tore me up inside, although I didn't let anyone know how I felt.

Through Cory, I met a boy named Dylan, and our alliance slowly grew after our mutual friend moved away. Thin and funny, Dylan reminded me of Samuel, so conversation soon came easily.

After weeks of silence, I finally felt comfortable talking about my Liberian background with a select group of people: Dylan, my neighbor Brenna, and eventually Shelby, a girl I met at camp. These friends accepted me for who I was and, most of all, I trusted them. They helped me get through my first days in America and they are still among my closest friends. Friendship had not failed me in Liberia and it was a source of security for me in this unfamiliar place.

Losing significant people in my life had opened plenty of space for me to welcome others in. Friends were the safest choice to fill that void.

NOW – 23

SCHOOL DAYS

School was another obstacle to overcome. I was one of the few black students in the building at the time, and I'm not just kind of black – *I'm really black* – so some people weren't sure what to think of me.

In most cases, my appearance turned out to be a good thing and I got a lot of attention, because I was a novelty. Kids would rub my hair to see how it felt, and although it drove me crazy, I never said a word to them. People were drawn to me as if I were a bright, shiny object; yet, in most cases, my response was guarded – unless, of course, I was being paid.

Still, I had a way of silently interacting with people that was somehow likeable. My dad calls it *quiet charisma*.

Learning to read and write was a difficult process. I hadn't attended first, second, or third grade, so when I was placed in fourth grade at about age nine, I had a lot of catching up to do. One of the neighbors my parents had introduced me to was Brenna's mom, Mrs. Palmer. She and another teacher, Mrs. Reinhart, patiently guided me through the difficult process of making up for lost time.

It wasn't easy, and in my most frustrating moments, I longed for the carefree lifestyle of the orphanage. I was confused because, in many ways, life in America was much harder than it was supposed to be. I vividly remember one day when I put my head down on a book and cried uncontrollably while some girls made fun of me.

This certainly was not the America I had dreamed of.

Yet, the teachers never gave up. When nothing else would work, Mrs. Palmer played *Go Fish* with me and it boosted my spirits. They put me in speech class and even a special education group, where I met one of my favorite teachers, Mrs. Whitaker.

While adding, subtracting and reciting the alphabet, I learned an equally important lesson about perseverance, and I owe a lot to the kind-hearted teachers who believed in me without hesitation.

NOW – 24

A GROWING FAMILY

The next several months were spent learning what it was like to be a brother to three American sisters, all very different from each other. Katie was six years older, and it was hard to connect with her until much later when she married DaWayne, a good-natured guy who loved to cook. When I told him that cooking was a woman's job, DaWayne said, "These days, women don't know how to cook, so you better learn." As it turns out, I think that was pretty good advice.

Kristin was at college in Myrtle Beach and we shared a love of sports along with a dry sense of humor. Although I didn't see her often, I could talk to Kristin with ease and we understood each other's jokes. Later, when I turned sixteen, Kristin sent me a driving helmet, and her simple, funny gesture made me feel like I was part of something. It reminded me of my days back in the orphanage when the mail delivery was the best part of the entire day.

Although Kelly and I are just two years apart, it seemed that we had the least in common. I loved sports; she was passionate about music. We expressed our differences by finding ways to get on each other's nerves. She'd flick my ear when I walked past and I'd make fun of her for sitting alone in her room. We became experts in the art of sibling rivalry.

Yet, more changes were in store, and soon after I settled in with this new family, my world was once more touched by adoption, although it wasn't my own. Less than a year after I arrived, our growing family expanded to include Ben (Prince), PJ (Princess), and John, three Liberian children who had traveled a similar path to America. My parents worked it out through a woman who made it her mission to connect Liberian orphans with families here in the states.

Although they had originally planned to adopt just two more children, my parents' unselfish decision to adopt all three was the only reason that siblings PJ and Ben would remain together rather than living with separate families. Actually, a family had already adopted Ben but things didn't work out, so if my parents had not come through, I don't know where he'd be today.

I remember the first time Ben came to our house, he was so excited at dinner that he grabbed the food from my plate and shoved it in his mouth. I don't think he had ever seen food like that before.

While my parents reprimanded Ben, I had to laugh as I remembered my first days here. There were times when I would open the refrigerator door and stare at the food – just to make sure it was still there.

Once, my dad made a huge pot of chili and rice and I couldn't get enough of it. When my parents asked me what I wanted for breakfast, I'd say, "Chili and rice." When the lunch question came, I responded, "Chili and rice." As the rest of the family settled in for a fish dinner, I filled up on chili and rice. I ate nothing but chili and rice for a solid month until I was finished with it. To this day, I've consumed enough chili and rice for the rest of my life.

While I tried to be happy for my new siblings, I was haunted by memories of Samuel, Playboy, and Momobah. My parents and I prayed for them each night and I wondered if they were okay. Truth be told, it made me angry to think that other kids were being adopted when I didn't even know where my closest friends were.

I hope they're still alive.

NOW – 25

NOT SO CLOSE KNIT

So, with new siblings in America – three older and three younger – I found myself right in the middle of things. I wasn't used to dealing with family at all, and now I had eight of them to manage between my parents, brothers, and sisters. Back in Liberia, family members nonchalantly stepped in and out of my life whenever they pleased. If I dared to get close to them, they avoided me, left, or died. Since then, I'd learned to put up a tough exterior that I wasn't planning to let any of these newfound relatives through.

I didn't know it at the time, but in the midst of everything else, my dad was battling cancer. Friends, neighbors, and church members helped us out when he was undergoing treatments, so I spent several weeks at Cory's house during that time. My dad handled his illness so well that I didn't understand what was going on until one day when he struggled while eating a spicy taco and my mom explained things to me.

Despite the heartache in my own life, seeing my dad's perseverance in such a traumatic situation was a striking reminder that difficult obstacles can be overcome. Although I was careful not to show it outwardly, I understood the value of faith and the power of prayer.

As a middle school student, I had plenty going on between homework, sports, and friends. Yet, there was a gaping hole in my heart from all the people I had lost in my life and I didn't know how to fill it. It seemed risky to become close with my family in America, because I was afraid something might happen to them. My solution was to become apathetic and sullen, retreating into my room as often as possible.

I spent a lot of time talking with people online, becoming close to a girl who was the friend of a friend. She confided in me about her deep sense of grief after losing siblings, saying she envied me. I stared blankly at my computer screen and thought of Jerry, my father, and even our little dog back in Liberia.

This girl and I had more in common than she realized. I was drawn to her words. They were a plea for help.

Eventually, she told me about her plans to commit suicide. As I listened to her speak honestly through written text, the emotions poured out of me and I started to believe that I had survived everything in my past for a reason. Most of all, I couldn't let someone else lose hope. Somehow, I found the words she needed to hear. Or maybe I just provided her with a sounding board where she could deposit her troubles and clear her mind enough to find her own heart in the middle of it all.

Although I didn't know it at the time, helping others became the key to unlocking some of the chambers in my own heart.

NOW – 26

WALLS, DOORS, AND EMPTY SPACES

Back at school, my confidence and friendships continued to grow, and I had the opportunity to participate on winning soccer and track teams. Sports opened doors for me, and after a lot of work and sacrifice, I became the champion of my weight class in wrestling, a proud accomplishment.

Increased success in sports brought additional friends, and little by little, I allowed those people through the wall and into that void in my heart. I talked often with Shelby, Dylan, Brenna, and Lauren, a girl I had met on Myspace. Lauren and I even dated for a few months until the start of school sent us off in different directions. We're still good friends and she's been there for me plenty of times when I needed someone to talk to.

As I had learned in Liberia, friends were my comfort. But I built up a barrier against my family and, at times, I was downright mean. I continued to make fun of Kelly when she read alone in her room and

I'm sorry to say that I encouraged our younger siblings to do the same. Despite my belligerence, my parents showed me nothing but love and support.

When I first came to America, my mom often carried me around in a large cloth wrapped close to her body, just like African mothers would do. During those early days, I longed for the safety of that cocoon.

As I grew older, my hunger for independence and a longing for understanding began to overtake my requirement for protection. My mother, a hospice nurse, responded to my change in spirit by hugging me more, and it began to drive me farther away. I know my mother wanted to hear me say, "I love you," but despite the warm feelings I had developed inside, I couldn't form the words. Would saying those words be a betrayal to my mother in Liberia? Did my birth mother ever hold me or love me?

Regardless of my friendships at school, the hole in my heart was still there. I slowly learned that I might be putting holes in other hearts, too.

NOW – 27

FORMING A BOND

My new brother, John, was dealing with emotional issues of his own. When he expressed his anger in ways people didn't understand, I was asked to help. Surprisingly, I sometimes found that I could. Although I talked to very few people at the time, I gave it my best because guilt was now joining forces with the fear in my life. I considered John's situation and had a nagging feeling that it was time for me to show I cared.

Often, I wasn't successful, and John kept fighting through my talking but I wanted to be there for him, even if sometimes it became physical. As I had learned in the orphanage, support is something you do for your friends. Little by little, I was beginning to understand that this feeling could be even stronger when it's your own brother.

John continued to deal with anger management issues for several years. Day after day, he fought with my dad and even with Mrs. Palmer as she kindly drove us to school amid it all.

Today, John has grown through most of it, but we learned a lot in the process and I'll always feel a special connection to him. During that time with John, I was reminded of Jerry and the incredible feeling I had when I first learned that I had a brother at the orphanage. I ached for that sense of brotherhood again. Even though it started out shaky, perhaps my experience with John was the first time I allowed myself to consider developing a true family bond in America.

Life is not about everything turning out perfectly or overcoming all obstacles to be a huge success. It's about putting yourself in the middle of things because you actually care enough to make them better.

Helping John allowed me to understand that.

NOW – 28

GOODBYE AGAIN

As a freshman at South River High School, I was excelling at sports. Yet, I continued to struggle academically and that created a lot of tension at home. Amid our heated conversations, my parents responded with unconditional love, something I didn't instantly recognize, or perhaps just wasn't ready to accept.

Exasperated with the situation, my parents checked out a few boarding schools in the area. We visited a variety of campuses, but it was the admissions officer at Randolph Macon Academy (RMA) who left an impression on me. He treated me like an adult, speaking frankly about my situation, and I became convinced that RMA was the answer I was looking for. Next thing I knew, I was enrolled at RMA, a boarding school located in Virginia, about two hours away.

Although the decision to attend RMA was partly mine, I couldn't help but feel that the circle was now complete. Family life in America had become nothing more than an extension of my days back in Liberia when I would visit Auntie Snoh for a while before she returned me to the orphanage.

No matter where I was, things never stood still. Life and movement became synonymous. It was clear that I didn't belong anywhere and even a trip to America couldn't change that. The only difference was that my latest abandonment was happening in a new place, one that was turning out to be far from heaven.

Before starting classes as a sophomore at RMA, I attended summer school where I met Collin and Nick. After class, we'd try to salvage some of the day by playing soccer and football out in the schoolyard. The RMA coach noticed my athletic skills and encouraged me to pursue football. I confided in Collin and Nick and they convinced me to go for it, so later that summer we would be together again at RMA's football camp.

Summer school dragged on and we longed for the end of class when we could hang out. One day, we went to the pool and met up with some girls we knew from summer school who did their best to get me to take my shirt off so they could see my eight-pack. I usually don't like to be the center of attention so I was reluctant to do it. Finally, I gave in and jumped up on the diving board to show off just a little. As it turned out, I tried a flip but slipped off the board, making everyone laugh. It was actually one of my favorite experiences.

Friends had become a necessity I couldn't live without.

NOW – 29

FINDING HOPE

When summer school was finally over, I escaped to three weeks at football camp where I met Seth, who was Collin's best friend. The three of us quickly became close but our fun was short-lived because it was only a matter of time before we'd all be engulfed in the busy world of RMA. I wondered if the admissions officer had played a trick on me by talking me into such a challenging place. The hole in my heart was filling, but unfortunately, resentment was taking up residence there.

Amid RMA's formal guidelines and military style, I encountered one of the most inspirational people I would ever come to know. Rebecca Quinn was my English teacher and she became like a mother to me in an environment that couldn't have been farther from home. Young, enthusiastic, and outgoing, Miss Quinn was a trusted mentor who took a genuine interest in me.

While some people at school seemed to judge me by my dark exterior, Miss Quinn got to know the *me* that was buried deep inside. I shared some of my history with her, and she recommended that I write a book about my life. Her words resonated in my mind, but at that point, I concluded that telling my story would only make people feel sorry for me. Pity was the last thing I wanted.

While at RMA, I could only go home once a month and my bitterness mounted. To compensate for time and distance, my parents sent me food and money. This added to my guilt because I already knew the school was an added expense for our family. My solution was to avoid talking to them at all, withdrawing farther inside my shell.

Life had become unbearably depressing, and there were many times when I contemplated suicide. I thought of the girl I used to talk to on the computer and couldn't believe I was slipping into such a dark place.

As I harbored dim feelings and negative thoughts, one of the few bright spots was Miss Quinn. When I had troubles that couldn't be resolved through texting with Dylan, Brenna, or Shelby, I went to Miss Quinn. She took the time to get to know each student, and in her class I felt freedom. I desperately needed a listening ear and this compassionate teacher became my lifeline.

While at RMA, I was devastated when a lovesick girlfriend tried to get my attention by cheating on me with one of my friends. The girl had succeeded in driving a wedge between one of my best buddies and me, and I was so furious that I refused to speak to her. She responded by cutting herself. I became extremely depressed and talked to Miss Quinn about the whole situation. When I was at a crossroad and ready to give up, she motivated me to keep going.

Quite simply, Rebecca Quinn gave me hope.

I remember a story Miss Quinn once told me about an elementary school student who attended her class when she worked in downtown Detroit. One day, the students were asked to draw a picture of *peace* and this young boy immediately went to work, angrily drawing a bold, black rectangle filled with more dark scribbles. At the time, one of the other teachers started to pull the student away from the group, reprimanding him for his wild actions. Miss Quinn insisted that the child be allowed to continue. After the pictures were finished, each student was asked to explain how his or her drawing showed peace. When it was his turn, the little boy explained the black box he had created, saying, "I think peace looks like the inside of my brother's coffin, because after he died, my aunt told me that he's now at peace."

I immediately thought of Jerry, and could finally feel a small sense of peace about it all.

There are very few adults in my life who get it, but Miss Quinn is one of them.

NOW – 30

YOU'VE GOT A FRIEND

As in other times of my life, it was friendship that carried me through my days at boarding school. During last period, Collin, Seth, Mike, Abraham, and I would sneak away to my room whenever we could to watch movies on the computer. One day, when the movie was over, we shared stories about how we had ended up at RMA, united by our difficult experiences.

Mike was a hefty guy who came from out west and, although he listened intently to our issues, he had trouble relaying his own. Uncomfortable, he laughed while we talked until he finally found the courage to explain his story through tear-filled eyes.

With heavy hearts, we hung on every word as Mike told us about the day he jumped through a window to help his frantic mom who was being beaten by his dad in their back yard. According to Mike, that day he picked up his dad, threw him across the lawn, and told him not to touch his mom again. His action got Mike a ticket to RMA, but we were all the better for it. Sitting there huddled in my tiny room, a bunch of tough guys learned that we all have feelings, and things are a lot easier when we allow caring people into our lives.

I tolerated boarding school by focusing on sports and hanging out with friends. I knew that the best way to improve at my sport was to challenge myself, so I targeted Trevor, one of the school's best athletes. He was faster than I was and I made it my goal to beat him in a footrace. After weeks of trying, I finally did just that and found true satisfaction in the hard-fought sense of accomplishment.

As it turned out, Trevor admired my effort and became like an older brother to me. It was proof that respect is earned more from genuine actions than mere words.

Back in the dorm, the guys liked to tease me about my African background. They'd ask me what it was like growing up in the jungle with lions and tigers. Although I'd never seen any of those animals – even in a zoo – I allowed their little African jokes because I knew it was their way of connecting with me.

I had another reason for tolerating their jokes. Back in Liberia, I had learned there is power in humor. I'll never forget the time at the orphanage when that high-ranking militant used a few jokes to silence the monsters who were attacking us in our little church. Humor actually saved lives that day. Perhaps that's why I've developed an inconspicuous laugh that comes in handy when I encounter sadness or trouble. Anyone who knows me well has heard it, but I doubt that they all understand it. That little chuckle allows me to hide my true feelings so people won't worry about me. It sends the message that I'm okay, buying me the time I need to figure things out on my own.

When we weren't in class or hanging out in the dorms, one of our favorite pastimes was going to town to meet the girls who were attracted to guys in uniform. At least those uncomfortable clothes served a useful purpose. Trevor, Chris, and I would often talk and laugh for hours on end at the local Chinese restaurant. Silly as they were, these light-hearted experiences were helping me through some of my darkest days.

Despite Miss Quinn and my friends, I still couldn't shake the depression I was feeling. After I threatened suicide several times, my parents finally gave in and brought me home for good.

Having escaped the rigors of boarding school, I quickly found myself in the midst of my next obstacle.

NOW – 31

TO BE OR NOT TO BE A GEEK

Miss Quinn, the teacher I so admired, had recommended that I go to Shakespeare Camp, of all things. One day in her class, we were reading Julius Caesar and, apparently, my rendition of Mark Antony had inspired her. She said I *became* him when I performed my speech. Miss Quinn insisted that she had never recommended anyone for this camp before and I was furious to be the first. Why would I want to spend my summer with geeky, artsy kids? In my world, camps were for sports, not theater.

My parents gave me two choices: summer school or Shakespeare camp. Camp seemed like the lesser of the two evils. Before I knew it, my friends were taking great pleasure in making fun of my most recent plight.

My first experiences at Shakespeare Camp were terrifying. I felt as alone on that stage as I had when I was three years old and standing in the middle of a dusty road. Now there were bright lights focused on me and I was nothing more than another tiny speck in an unfamiliar place. Even worse, there were people in the audience, and many others sitting right on the stage. Prior to this, I had barely spoken to anyone other than my friends; yet, at this camp, I was expected to involve people in my performance. I felt betrayed by the mentor I had come to respect.

So I again leaned on friendship, the reliable pillar that had remained steadfast through anything life had to offer. I became close friends with Baxter, a surfer type who was pursued by all the good-looking girls at camp. We were like brothers, going everywhere together, and other people said they wished they had our kind of friendship. Practicing lines six hours a day and hanging out with Baxter gave me time to develop both confidence and camaraderie.

The lines weren't so bad once I realized that Shakespeare's characters and I had something in common. We were each okay with being the butt of the joke if that's what it took to make people laugh.

Shakespeare Camp rekindled memories of days at the orphanage when Russia King cast us in plays to help pass the time. Then, as now, I learned life lessons along the way. At camp, I developed an amazing connection with my character, who happened to be the hero in "Richard III."

It took a while, but somewhere in the middle of learning how to convincingly deliver 37 lines about slaying a villain, I discovered a lot about shedding my own fears.

When camp ended, I took home much more than I had brought with me. I owe it to people like Miss Quinn and my parents who saw more in me than I was able to find in myself at the time.

NOW – 32

ANCHORS AWEIGH

Our home was located about twenty minutes from the Naval Academy in Annapolis where Midshipmen came from all over the country to learn about leadership and honor. Since many of the Midshipmen were far from their roots, the Academy initiated a sponsorship program to provide them with a home away from home during their education. My parents were thrilled to take part, sponsoring a Midshipman named James.

James was like an older brother to me. I still consider him a role model. Even though I was smaller than James, I liked to wrestle him because I found that, occasionally, I could actually beat him. I was reminded of how I had become a better runner by taking on a superstar like Trevor, so I was intrigued by this new challenge.

One of my favorite memories was when we went to Virginia Beach where James was stationed after graduation. Late one night, we ran out on the beach to wrestle in the sand. With our adrenalin at a peak and sand flying everywhere, it was just like the scuffles I had experienced with friends back at the orphanage. The harder we fought, the more we laughed. I'm not really sure who won but it took me weeks to get the sand out of my dreadlocks.

My most memorable moment with James was when we were hanging out at my house just before he left for a tour in Japan. We loved to trash talk and pick on each other.

That night, our taunts escalated until we burst through the door and ran out into the pouring rain. As the water beat down on us, our intensity increased, and it didn't matter anymore who won. What actually mattered was the respect we had for each other as athletes and friends. When we came back inside, soaking wet and out of breath, we fell into our chairs and talked until 2:00 in the morning.

To this day I still admire him.

NOW – 33

FINDING GRACE IN DISGRACE

Spending that time with James and learning about the sense of duty and respect he has for America reminds me of my homeland so far away. By settling into a comfortable American life without maintaining traditional customs, I feel that I've become a disgrace to my African heritage. It seems like I've embraced American ways at the expense of my own roots.

Although my parents always encouraged me to honor my background – even studying Liberian customs and occasionally wearing native clothing of their own – I did very little to share in those activities. When they invited a Liberian couple to our home, I hid in my room, ashamed that I couldn't understand my native language.

The small jar of Blue Magic, a mask, and some clothes are all I have to remind me of my African heritage. I never took the time to learn about the Kru customs or practice the tone systems that would connect me to my birthplace, and I have no one to blame but myself.

I am always confused when people refer to every black person as an African American. Unless they were born in Africa, I think of blacks as simply Americans, the same way we'd refer to American-born people of German descent. Since I was born in Africa, I consider myself an African, just as a person born in Germany would be German. Given my dual citizenship, the term African-American works for me, too.

The older I get, the more I realize that my connection with Africa is not about labels or clothing or languages. It's about the person I am becoming. I believe that the African spirit is characterized by a respect for others and an appreciation for the simple things in life. In the midst of privileges such as computers, cell phones, and TV, I need to remind myself of the sharing and generosity I learned as a young child in a caring orphanage.

No matter where I go, the essence of Africa will live inside me, and that gives me a strong sense of pride. While in Liberia, I took on these humble, native characteristics in the same way a seedling absorbs nutrients from the soil.

I did nothing to earn this unique gift, and tending it is an incredible responsibility.

NOW – 34

MAKING MY WAY

While I was relieved to be away from the disciplined atmosphere of boarding school, I found myself right back on the familiar turnstile. Life at home was still tenuous as we dealt with the pressures of grades, social issues, and all the challenges that come with an evolving family.

After much research, it was decided that my next stop would be Archbishop Curley, a private school in Baltimore where I could develop academically and athletically. My first response at the thought of attending an all-boys school was negative, and although my friend Lauren provided encouragement, I didn't appreciate her support until months later.

At Curley, I started off in the Anthony program, a base level curriculum that would allow me to acclimate as needed. The classes were fairly easy, although I had a lot of homework, especially in my religion class. Raised in a Lutheran home here in America, I would ask the friar to elaborate on things I didn't understand about the

Catholic Church, taking great pleasure in challenging concepts that were contrary to my beliefs. For example, I wouldn't go to confession because I don't believe that other humans can provide absolution. The way I see it, only God can do that. My church-centered upbringing in both Liberia and America was proving to be helpful as I made my own way in the world.

On the athletic front, I made the junior varsity soccer team at Curley and scored five goals in my first season. I became friends with a lot of guys on the team, although it took time because I had specific methods for getting to know people. When I first encountered someone, I would act intimidating, refusing to talk or smile. It was my way of commanding respect and testing the waters until I could develop trust. Once people realized I wouldn't tolerate nonsense, all the walls came down and friendships formed.

My closest friends quickly learned that I'm really a big teddy bear, and we amused ourselves by making fun of each other. I had to laugh at the backhanded compliment I received from one of my buddies, who proudly told me I wasn't like all the other "darkies." By this time, I was used to the ribbing; I had heard it all from the guys back at RMA.

Later that fall, I received a text from Shelby, asking me to go with her to homecoming at Severn, where she attended school. We were always good friends but her last-minute request caught me by surprise. We had just three days to make plans.

After we finalized the details of what to wear and the color of her corsage, I decided to get my hair cut. I hadn't been to an official barber for quite some time, and when he asked what type of cut I wanted, I looked at the guy in front of me and said, "I'll take what he's getting."

Later that night, I was the baldest guy at homecoming, sporting the same shaved head style I had so many years ago at the orphanage.

As usual, I laughed the hardest at myself and we had a great time.

NOW – 35

WRESTLING WITH LIFE

With soccer season over, I focused my attention on wrestling where I met more friends. One of them was James, who was also African. James and I bonded through our common background and he liked to tease me about the fact that I spoke "all proper like an American." I shot back that he talked the same way, and we laughed at the ordinary people we had become despite our extraordinary backgrounds. Our innocent rivalry often played out in the locker room, and I still have a back injury from the time I mistakenly thought I was a superhero who could pick James up and drop him to the floor.

I also became friends with a wrestler named Fred. I guess I was his "Trevor" because he liked to challenge himself by trying to out-wrestle me, something he only did twice.

Another close friend was Avery, one of the school's top athletes who excelled at football, track and wrestling. When I first met Avery, I was intimidated by the fact that he was an athletic legend, but he challenged me to wrestle him because he had heard I was pretty good. I refused his offer in laughter and didn't compete with him until we had become good friends.

My favorite wrestling move was the gator roll and I liked to do it from the standing position because that was more efficient, even though it's riskier. I would get my opponent in a headlock, trap his arm, and spin and flip him until I took him down.

I can't say I ever beat Avery, but I'm proud of the fact that I was able to take him down a few times and he didn't pin me. Avery definitely made me a more effective competitor, and he continued to be my role model as he headed off to Temple University on a football scholarship. Going up against people who were bigger and stronger only made me better.

I guess life can be that way, too.

Wrestling with tough obstacles can shape you into something good.

NOW – 36

RUNNING THE RACE

My life and friendships at Curley revolved around sports seasons, and track was next in line. I didn't expect to make the varsity team because Curley had a lot of talented athletes. Those tryouts made me especially nervous since I had never run for a great track team. Sure, I had laced up my running shoes at RMA, but Curley was in a class of its own. Surprisingly, I made the team and ran in individual sprints and relays.

My relay teammates often blamed me for any problems we encountered since I had the least amount of experience. I had to work hard on my starts, and it took hours of practice to finally get the timing right. Slowly, I developed my skill and earned the trust of the team. Yet, the competition was fierce and every meet was a huge challenge.

One time, during the 4x100 in Annapolis, another runner accidentally knocked the baton out of my hand. I had to run back to get it, sacrificing valuable time. If it weren't for this mishap, we would have easily won the race. We were furious, and when it was all over, the kid who bumped into me came back and apologized so we wouldn't beat him up.

Although the 400 was not my event, a relay team member had failed to show up for one of the meets so I was asked to fill in at the last minute. Having never run the 400 in an official race, I got off to a slow start. Ultimately, I kicked into full gear and ran a 0.53, which was the fastest leg for my team. Although I knew I could do it, I had been holding out, because I didn't want to run the 400. Let's face it, that event is downright grueling, and it feels like a marathon sprint. After I saved the relay that day, my secret was out and the coaches made it clear that, like it or not, the 400 would be mine to run.

That year, our track team beat every opponent we were up against except Gilman. We lost to them in the conference tournament, leaving us in second place.

In addition to earning the respect of my teammates during that season, I learned that it wasn't fair to hold back when I had something to give – even if it meant doing something hard.

It's usually the hard things in life that are most worth the effort.

NOW – 37

DECIDING FACTORS

Another teammate, Dino, became one of my best friends. Small and kind, Dino was like a younger brother who reminded me of Samuel. To alleviate the long drive to Baltimore, I stayed with Dino's family for several weeks, so we had plenty of time to hang out and joke with each other. I spent most of my weekdays at Dino's house, returning home only on weekends. Like Auntie Snoh, Dino's grandma was a great cook. Her pasta could brighten a rainy day.

But I couldn't stay with Dino's family forever and the long drive to Baltimore didn't fit into our family's schedule now that my mom had a new job. The only way I could attend Curley in my junior year was if I could get my driver's license, although my mom still didn't like the idea of someone with my limited experience navigating the busy streets of Baltimore. It didn't help that my sister Kelly recently had been involved in a minor car accident.

Driving was a huge obstacle but I wanted to overcome it because going to Curley meant the world to me. The most terrifying part about driving a car was the possibility that, if I screwed up, I could hurt or kill someone else. That scared me to death.

So far, my concerns about driving haven't mattered, because the test is an obstacle I have yet to overcome. The first time I took it, the evaluator started talking to me while I was driving, and the distraction made it impossible to concentrate.

Leaving Curley was one of the hardest things I've had to do since I moved to America. The school challenged me academically and athletically and I knew that both of those things were good for me.

Yet, sometimes, our circumstances determine our path in life more than our desires. In my case, something as basic as transportation became a deciding factor.

I had no choice but to make the most of it.

NOW – 38

MAKING THE MOST OF IT, AGAIN

I had attended South River High School before, and the wrestling coach always said I could come back to the team anytime. On the day of tryouts, I was unable to take part due to a medical appointment, and the coach also noticed that I had failed to turn in some required paperwork. I guess he added all that up in his head and came to the conclusion that I had lost my enthusiasm for the sport. That meant I couldn't join the team.

Without a word, I grabbed my stuff and walked out.

As the school year went on, I searched for friendships that would get me through. I eventually joined the track team where my childhood buddy, James, introduced me to Conor and John. I also reconnected with Josh, a teammate I knew from soccer many years earlier.

Josh and I loved to challenge each other because we're both athletic. I would remind him of my chiseled eight-pack; he would counter with the fact that he ran the 400 in 0.56, compared with 0.57, my best time so far at South River. It was all in good fun and I'm grateful to my teammates for their friendship. In fact, I wouldn't have been able to participate in sports at all if it weren't for them driving me to and from practices. Our family had more kids and activities than drivers to go around – especially since I still didn't have my license.

Although I was enjoying track, I couldn't shake the fact that I had walked out on my wrestling coach earlier in the year. It wasn't like me to do that and I knew it involved more than just sports. To many people, it probably looked like I gave up. Looking back, I think the coach had noticed a change in me, and perhaps he was encouraging me to figure things out.

My enthusiasm hadn't diminished, but my priorities were shifting.

The difficult move from Curley to South River was forcing me to confront unfinished business in my life. Despite the genuine brotherhood I had developed with so many friends, I couldn't keep hiding inside the comfort of sports teams unless I came to terms with the bigger issues of connecting with my family and tending to the hole that continued to exist in my heart.

I was still harboring a lot of anger over leaving a school that meant so much to me. Trying to make sense of it, I leaned on my friends Emma and Erin, whose support never wavered through all my darkest moods. Their smiles helped me find happiness again.

Once the happiness resurfaced, I finally realized that something was pulling me home.

Home. Maybe I'm beginning to understand what that truly means.

NOW – 39

CONTINUING THE CLIMB

Looking back on the time in Liberia and my relationships with Samuel, John, Playboy, and Momobah, I realize what made me a good friend. When others were wrestling with challenges, I was able to listen without missing the details, to speak only the words that needed to be said, and most of all, just to be there when I was needed.

Those same characteristics were leading me into strong friendships in America. When I trusted a person, I shared a piece of my background, and that simple honesty opened a door that most people were comfortable walking through.

I've come to realize that all the movement in my life has been a benefit, opening doors, providing opportunity, and giving me a voice in the world. Most of all, the journey introduced me to caring people who built my character.

At the orphanage, Pastor Sieh and his wife and Russia King established my faith. Compassion came from Auntie Snoh. Old friends like Playboy, Samuel, and Momobah helped me earn respect, while my new friends in America shared trust. Mrs. Palmer and Mrs. Whitaker taught me about perseverance. Thousands of miles apart, my brothers Jerry and John gave me two unique views of brotherhood. Midshipman James showed me about honor and a sense of duty. Rebecca Quinn took the time to know the real me, offering the precious gift of hope. And my mom and dad here in America introduced me to the incredible concept of unconditional love – in addition to helping me completely overcome my fear of water.

Despite all the progress, I'm still working on developing a strong connection with my new family, and I want so much to make it happen. I can't fill the hole in my heart without them, but they can't enter in unless I move the wall. My sister Kelly continues to drive me where I need to go, despite the way I've treated her in the past. My younger siblings look up to me and I need to be there for them.

I've built a solid relationship with my dad who somehow overcame cancer in the middle of everything I threw at him. Although I never come out and say it, I admire his strength and especially value his work ethic.

I'm still learning how to connect with my mom. A mother's love is different from any other love in terms of intensity and expression. When you have that mother-child affection from birth, it becomes part of you, and it's the most natural thing in the world. When you encounter such love after you've been running around on your own for nine years, it's another thing altogether. It's harder to grasp, and although it must be the most amazing feeling on earth, I haven't completely warmed up to it yet.

Sometimes the intensity of that mother-son emotion is unbearable because I'm experiencing it from the outside-in, rather than from the inside-out as most people do. The bottom line is that this is one of the biggest deals in my life. Even though I can't force the feelings, I'll take whatever time is needed to get there.

It's all part of growing up.

I'm not sure exactly how to do it, but it's my turn to give back. I'm starting to view that hole in my heart as an opportunity rather than a void. It's amazing how losing people throughout your life can actually open up room for you to let others in.

Scars in our lives are blessings when we look at them through faith-filled eyes. The scar on my forehead, just below my hairline, provides a daily reminder of the brother who gave me the courage to take a risk for the sake of family.

And that's when it hit me. More than anything, I need to show my new family how much I love and appreciate them.

NOW – 40

BACK IN THE MIDDLE

I'd imagine most people have something that haunts them: perhaps a mistake, worry or regret. For me, it was fear. It surrounded me in some form or another just about every day while I was living in Liberia and fear followed me to America.

The key is that I didn't let fear get *inside* me, and in the end, fear didn't shape me. I was molded by people who showed me how to love in the middle of turmoil and by a faith that always appeared when I needed it most.

Fear is like those tough guys on my sports teams who made me better and stronger when I challenged them. I've wrestled with fear, and although I won't say I've pinned it to the mat, I've definitely beaten it on several occasions.

That effort helped me to grow.

In the Middle of the Line

People think strength comes from being first. For me, it has always come from being in the middle – at the heart of what matters.

In Liberia, I met people who had lost limbs; in America, I've met people who've lost hope. Because of my experience, I'll never be one of them. I'm too busy looking ahead to see what I can learn from those in front of me, and reaching back to pull others forward.

My story ends in the middle. I'm in the middle of wrestling big things, facing fears, building trust, removing guilt, and filling that gaping hole in my heart.

Perhaps I've inspired you, too.

Baruch Talbott and Debby Coughlan

EPILOGUE

I believe that everything happens for a reason because God has the power to give and take away life in order to create opportunities and mend broken hearts and promises. Throughout my life, I've lost many things: my parents, my older brother, and some of my closest friends. I've lost hope and faith in God. I even lost my desire to continue on living after so many people stepped out of my life at such a young age.

As a child I couldn't comprehend what was going on but now that I've grown up and matured a bit, I understand that God took away my parents, older bother and some of my closest friends whom I loved dearly to open windows and opportunities for me. As I've lived in America for the last nine years of my life, I've seen and felt the presence of some of the people I've lost in the faces of my new friends and family in America.

I believe I am here today to tell the story of our epic journey and sad ending for some of my brothers and sisters. Although death has sealed their lips, their story will be heard through mine. Their life and death has made me strong mentally, emotionally, and physically. It has helped me become mature, understanding, and more appreciative. They have helped me realize that every breath and step I take is a gift from God.

My ambition in life is to reach out to those who have lost hope and faith, to be a listening ear to those who have a story to tell, and to inspire others to tell their stories.   -- Baruch

Baruch Talbott and Debby Coughlan

REFERENCES

AllAfrica.com. 2006. *Liberia: Fallen Associate Justice Remembered.* Retrieved August 29, 2012 from http://allafrica.com/stories/200607120451.html

The Daily Beast, Newsweek. 2012. Geoffrey Robertson, contributor. *Awaiting a verdict in Charles Taylor's war crimes trial.* Retrieved August 24, 2012 from http://www.thedailybeast.com/newsweek/2012/04/15/awaiting-a-verdict-in-charles-taylor-s-war-crimes-trial.html

The Daily Beast. Newsweek. 2012. Leymah Gbowee, contributor. *A dictator, vanquished.* Retrieved August 24, 2012 from http://www.thedailybeast.com/newsweek/2012/ 04/29/a-dictator-vanquished.html

"Liberia." *The World Book Encyclopedia.* 2011. Print.